THE
TEN COMMANDMENTS
OF GOD

THE
TEN COMMANDMENTS
OF GOD

By:
Rev. Albert Joseph Mary Shamon

CMJ MARIAN PUBLISHERS & DISTRIBUTORS
P.O. Box 661
Oak Lawn, Illinois 60454
www.cmjbooks.com
(708) 636-2995

Nihil Obstat: Rev. William E. Graf
                   September 8, 1995
                   Rochester, NY
                   Censor

The *Nihil Obstat* and *Imprimatur* are a declaration that a book or pamphlet is to be considered to be free from doctrinal or moral error. It is not implied that those who have granted the *Nihil Obstat* and *Imprimatur* agree with the contents, opinions or statements expressed.

Imprimatur: ✠ Matthew H. Clark
                 Bishop of Rochester, NY
                 September 11, 1995

Published by CMJ Marian Publishers

For additional copies write:

CMJ Marian Publishers & Distributors
P.O. Box 661
Oak Lawn, Illinois 60454
www.cmjbooks.com

Individuals may acquire additional copies through your local religious bookstore, or by contacting the publisher.

ISBN: 1-891280-16-3

Library of Congress Catalog Card No.: 00-102930

All biblical references were taken from the NEW AMERICAN BIBLE, St. Joseph Personal Size Edition.

Printed in the United States.

Contents

Page

Preface vii

Chapter 1
Why did God give us the Ten Commandments? 1

Chapter 2
Why must I worship God? 3

Chapter 3
Why must I pray? 5

Chapter 4
Why is it wrong to be superstitious? 8

Chapter 5
Why is it wrong to use profanity? 11

Chapter 6
Why is it wrong to miss Mass deliberately
on Sunday? 14

Chapter 7
Why is it wrong to do unnecessary work on Sunday? 18

Chapter 8
Why must we love, honor, and obey our parents? 22

Chapter 9
Why is it wrong to take the life of another
on my own authority? 25

Chapter 10
Why are abortion and euthanasia wrong? 29

Chapter 11
Why is it wrong to commit adultery? 33

Chapter 12
Why the sexes? Why sex? 36

Chapter 13
Why is it wrong to covet your neighbor's wife? 40

Chapter 14
Why is it wrong to steal? 43

Chapter 15
Why is it wrong to covet your neighbor's goods? 46

Chapter 16
Why is it wrong to tell lies? 49

Chapter 17
Epilogue 53

Preface

When the courts of this country banned the posting of the Ten Commandments in classrooms and public buildings, I was appalled and angered.

Such idiocy. Separation of Church and State, they call it, as though morality were a church. One might just as well ban the teaching of the Law of Gravity from the classroom on the grounds that it was discovered by a Jew, Sir Isaac Newton. Or restrict the teaching of the Law of Relativity only to the synagogue, because it too was discovered by a Jew, Albert Einstein. Because the Ten Commandments come to us through a Jew, Moses, it's religion—and so to be banned? Hogwash! Balderdash! Tommyrot!

In Auburn, New York, we reacted against this unreasonable ruling of our courts in a twofold manner. First, the P.R.A.Y.E.R.S. Apostolate in Auburn has published posters of the Ten Commandments to be hung in the classrooms of Catholic schools and in homes and businesses. (These may be obtained from Frank Scucces, 18 Crescent Avenue, Auburn, New York 13021, Ph. 315/252-1653.)

The second reaction is this little booklet on the Ten Commandments. However, I have written it from the viewpoint of common sense and good reason. In other words, I have taken each commandment and asked the question, "Why?" Why must I pray? Why must I honor my father and my mother? Why can't I kill? Why can't I steal? Why can't I lie, and so on. And I have sought to answer most of these questions from reason alone. My aim is to show that the Ten

Commandments are rooted in common sense and good judgment; that they are basically justice and rights; that they defend the dignity of man and woman and are geared to protecting parents, life, spouse, property, and reputation; that a nation committed to law and order is committing civil euthanasia by outlawing the Ten Commandments from the public forum.

To deprive our youth of these Ten Commandments on the questionable grounds of separation of Church and State is like taking a road map away from one traveling in a foreign land; or like smashing the compass on a liner.

We decry the violence in our land, the lawlessness of our youth. We have killed the piper and lament we have no music.

We must not only give God back to our nation, but we must also give His laws back to our nation if we would save it. Who does not give heed to the rudder will soon give heed to the rocks.

Feasts of the Sacred Heart of Jesus
and the Immaculate Heart of Mary
June 24, 1995

Chapter 1

Why did God give us the Ten Commandments?

Suppose you were traveling through a woods, and you lost your way. Suppose then you came across a woodsman who knew the way you should go to reach your home. What would you do? What would he do? You would ask him for directions, and he would give them to you.

All of us are traveling through the woods of this world to our home in Heaven. To guide us we have our reason. But as so often has happened in history, we can lose our way. We can get all mixed up.

That is what happened to God's people in Egypt. The Egyptians were pagans; they worshipped false gods and goddesses. God's people lived among them for 400 years. And what happened? Sure enough they were affected by the errors all around them. These rubbed off on them so that they lost their sense of right and wrong, of good and evil. So when Moses led them out of Egypt, God had to give them directions as to what was right and what was wrong. On Mount Sinai, He did just that: He gave their leader, Moses, the Ten Commandments.

It is significant that God never gave the patriarchs the Ten Commandments. Why? Because they seldom lost their sense of what was right and what was wrong. When Joseph was in Egypt and Putiphar's wife tried to get him to sin with her, he refused. He knew it was wrong, and he was willing to face imprisonment and death rather than sin.

Today, we, like God's people in Egypt, have lost our way.

So many make themselves the judge of what is right and what is wrong. So many condone hideous sins today, like abortion, artificial contraception, homosexual and lesbian acts, greed, malice, spite. They are insolent, haughty, ingenious in their wickedness, and rebellious toward their parents. They are senseless, heartless, ruthless, and even approve these evils in others. That is why it is so important to go back to the Ten Commandments. We've lost our way. Too many are taking the wrong road: the road to Hell and not the road to Heaven.

Like a good woodsman, God has given us directions. If one lost in the woods would not listen to the woodsman who knows the way out, he would be foolish. So are we, if we in our arrogance reject God's directions and depend only on ourselves.

Read: *Matthew* 5:17-19.

Chapter 2

Why must I worship God?

Worship simply means to acknowledge the **worth** of another. We're always doing that. When an athlete makes a great play in baseball or football, don't we all cheer? When an actor or actress gives a four-star performance, isn't he or she given an Oscar? When great tenors, like Luciano Pavorotti, Placido Domingo, Jose Carrera, thrill audiences with favorite arias, don't we give them standing ovations?

One more thing. Suppose you wanted to become a great athlete or actor or singer, wouldn't you try to imitate your "idol"? Wouldn't you, if you could, get their advice and follow it gladly? Wouldn't you, if you could, ask their help? Wouldn't you make the sacrifices they tell you are needed to reach your goal? Of course you would.

Then why should it be different when it comes to God? No star, no idol, can even come close to Him. With a single word, He created this most wonderful world for us. Every day and every hour He is constantly heaping countless blessings on us. He even sent His Son to save us.

One day a man came to St. Francis of Assisi and asked him why he should love God or worship Him? St. Francis said nothing, but took the man down the street to where a crippled blind beggar was sitting. Francis went up to the man and said, "Sir, if I give you your sight and restore your health, would you love me?"

"Love you!" exclaimed the beggar. "Why I'd be your slave for life." Francis cured him. Then he turned to his doubter and said, "God has given you your sight and your wealth and all that you are and have, and you say you cannot love him?"

Worship God? We should idolize Him (that is **adoration**). We should eagerly follow His directions (that is **devotion**). We should ask His help (that is **prayer**). We should take up the cross daily in order to follow Christ (that is **sacrifice**). Doesn't all that make sense?

Well, that is all worship is—to adore God, to be devoted to God, to pray to Him, to make sacrifices for Him. To do all this is to be religious. Sometimes we don't quite understand what religion is. Often, I have asked the question: "What is the object of religion?" You know, I seldom get a correct answer.

The object of religion is a **debt** we owe God. That is why St. Thomas put religion under the virtue of justice. Justice simply means to give to another that which is due. If you owe a bill, you pay it. That's justice. In the Preface of the Mass we say: "It is right always and everywhere to give thanks to God." In the old Latin Mass the words "and just" were there. "It is right **and just** always and everywhere to give thanks to God."

Worship is nothing more than paying our bills. We owe God! We owe Him for our life, our livelihood, our faith, our well-being. We owe Him for everything we have and are. To the Athenians St. Paul said: *"It is He who gives to everyone life and breath and everything"* (*Acts* 17:25). Then to the Corinthians he asked: *"What do you possess that you have not received? But if you have received it, why are you boasting as if you did not receive it?"* (*1 Cor.* 4:7).

To deny God worship—the honor, love and service due Him—is to welch on a debt. We idolize our heroes. But as St. Michael the Archangel said when he cast Lucifer out of Heaven, *"Who is like unto God?"*

Chapter 3

Why must I pray?

Prayer is not a fawning on God, coaxing Him to play favorites, wheedling Him to change His mind. We pray because God has decreed not only **what** will happen but **why** it will happen. God has made prayer a cause. Our God, who said that unless you sow seed, you shall not have a harvest, also said that, unless you pray, you are not going to get certain important things.

God, for instance, gives us many things without our asking Him, but there are certain other things that He will not give us without our asking Him—namely, our salvation. As St. Augustine said, "He who created us without our consent will not save us without our consent."

And why does God do this? Precisely to help us save ourselves. The greatest danger to our salvation lies in our tendency to declare our independence of God. Were everything given us without our asking, we, proud-bent as we are, would soon think ourselves lord and master of all things; and, puffed up with pride, we would fall from grace like Lucifer. That is the great pitfall of the New Age movement of today.

Prayer is the oxygen of the soul. As the body dies without oxygen, so the soul dies without prayer.

So important is prayer that St. Alphonsus Ligouri said: "If I had only one sermon to preach in my whole life it would be on prayer"—for if you pray, you will be saved; but if you do not pray, you will certainly be lost."

We pray, therefore, not to change God's will, but to change ourselves to conform to God's will.

We pray, not to change God, but to change ourselves.

We pray, not to reveal our needs to God, but to reveal to ourselves our need for God.

Prayer opens up our hearts. Take a flower or plant. Water it daily, and eventually it will blossom into a beautiful flower. Prayer is water to the heart. Water the heart daily with prayer and it too will grow and blossom like a beautiful flower. Without the water of prayer, our hearts will shrivel up, become sterile, and die to the things of God.

There are at least three times we should pray: morning, night, and in times of temptation.

Don't let "saying" prayers get in the way of your praying. In the morning simply fall to your knees, make the Sign of the Cross, and say, "Good morning, Jesus. Thanks for the good night's sleep. I offer this day to You. Please be with me today." That is all. In the morning all a husband has to say to his wife at breakfast is, "Good morning, Honey. Did you have a good sleep? I love you." That's all. Those few words would make her day.

At night, again fall to your knees, make the Sign of the Cross and say, "Thank you, Jesus, for the blessings of this day." (Name a blessing.) Then tell Him you are sorry for any lapse that might have occurred that day. (Name one.) And finally, ask Him to give you a good night's sleep and, should you die, to take you to Heaven.

Just as the hem on a dress keeps it from unraveling, so morning and night prayers will keep your day from unraveling.

In time of temptation, simply run to Jesus or Mary and breath a short pray, like "Jesus and Mary help me." They will. Never was it known that anyone who fled to their protection was left unaided.

If you pray well, you'll live well;
If you live well, you'll die well;
If you die well, you won't go to Hell;
And if you don't go to Hell, then all is well.

Chapter 4

Why is it wrong to be superstitious?

Superstition means to seek help or favor by inadequate ways and means; to seek an effect without a proportionate cause—for instance, to think a rabbit's foot will bring good luck or the number 13 will bring bad luck.

Superstition is stupid foolishness, because one seeks an effect without a proper cause. Take the number 13. You can read it either way.

Some will say 13 brings bad luck. Christ and His apostles numbered 13, one fell. Constantinople fell in 1453 (1+4+5+3=13); and the emperor at the time was Constantine the 13th.

But we can also say that 13 is good luck. The United States began with 13 colonies. The great seal of the United States on the back of a one-dollar bill has 13 stars, 13 stripes, 13 arrows in the eagle's talon, 13 clouds in the glory, 13 letters in the motto *e pluribus unum*, 13 laurel leaves, 13 berries in the branch, 13 feathers in each wing, and 13 feathers in the tail. Is a dollar bill bad luck?

The use of sacramentals, like scapulars, medals, rosaries, and so on, is not superstition, because sacramentals seek an effect through a proportionate cause, namely, through the prayers of the Church and the faith of the recipients.

The evil thing about being superstitious is that it denies the providence of God. Jesus said, *"Are not two sparrows sold for a small coin? Yet not one of them falls to the ground without your Father's knowledge. Even all the hairs of your head are counted"* (*Matthew* 10:29-30). In the words of Hamlet: "There's a divinity that shapes our ends,/ Rough-hew them how we will." God's got the whole world in His hands. Our role is to trust God, not other persons or things.

Instead of trusting in God, some put their trust in human persons, living or dead. Some seek to know the future by cards, palmistry, astrology.

Shakespeare, in *Macbeth*, shows the terrible consequences of believing in witches. Three witches greeted Macbeth after his victory over the enemies of King Duncan of Scotland. They hailed him as thane of Glamis, thane of Cawdor, then with the words, "Thou shalt be king hereafter."

When Banquo, Macbeth's friend, saw the effect this prediction about becoming king had on Macbeth, he warned him saying, " . . . but 'tis strange;/ And oftentimes, to win us to our harm,/ The instruments of darkness tell us truths,/ Win us with honest trifles, to betray's/ In deepest consequence." And that was precisely what happened. Macbeth was destroyed in the end.

Some seek knowledge through contact with the dead, through table rappings, the mouth of a medium, automatic writing, or the ouija board.

The ouija board gets it name from the French word for "yes," *oui*, and the German word for "yes," *ja.* Playing with this "yes-yes" thing can be dangerous, because you might get a correct answer through coincidence or because an evil spirit knows many future things, as can a doctor because of his knowledge know that a patient has only a few months to live. A correct answer from a ouija board could weaken one's faith.

Scripture says: *"Let there not be found among you . . . a fortune-teller, soothsayer, charmer, diviner, or caster of spells, nor one who consults ghosts and spirits or seeks ora-*

cles from the dead . . . . Anyone who does such things is an abomination to the Lord" (*Deuteronomy* 18:10-12).

We must remember that the future does not exist. Only God knows the future. Over the future there is a "No Trespassing" sign. To trespass into the future brings only worry and fear. Thus Jesus said: *"Sufficient for a day is its own evil"* (*Matthew* 6:34). In the words of Henry Wadsworth Longfellow:

> Trust no Future, howe'er pleasant!
> Let the dead Past bury its dead!
> Act—act in the living Present!
> Heart within, and God o'erhead!

Chapter 5

Why is it wrong to use profanity?

Profanity means to take the name of the Lord our God in vain. That simply means using God's name or the name of Jesus, not in prayer or praise, but to express anger or surprise or emphasis. To do that is like burning the American flag or desecrating the Lincoln Memorial.

Words are powerful. God created the world with a word. By the words of consecration, a priest can bring Christ to our altars on earth at every Mass. By the words of absolution, a priest can forgive the most scarlet of sins. God Himself attaches such power to words.

One of the most powerful words in the world is the word **"Jesus."** Jesus Himself promised: *"If you ask anything of me in my name, I will do it"* (*John* 14:14). It is the name that makes the dying live, that gives the blind their sight. In the name of Jesus, Peter cured a man crippled from birth (*Acts* 3). *"At the name of Jesus,"* said St. Paul, *"every knee should bend, of those in Heaven and on earth and under the earth"* (*Philippians* 2:10).

To desecrate that name is folly. Before the Kimberly mines were discovered in South Africa, natives used diamonds for their slingshots. They did not know the worth of diamonds. But to know the power of the name of Jesus and then to use it in profanity, what excuse can one have?

George Washington, when he heard that profanity was being used in the army, issued a scathing denunciation of this practice in 1776. He wrote to his officers in the Continental Army, "I hope that you will by word and example endeavor to check this folly. For how can we hope for the blessings of God on our arms if we insult Him by this impiety. Profanity is a vice so mean and low, without any temptation, that every man of sense and character detests and despises it."

Why, then, do people swear?

Psychiatrists agree that they do this because they have an odd quirk in their personality: a feeling of inferiority and some emotional immaturity.

Thus some swear from peer pressure. They want to be accepted by their peer group. They feel that profanity makes them appear tough and hairy, brawny and hard. Profanity is no more a sign of manliness than are dirty fingernails, unbrushed teeth, or a dirty face. Ragged dress is the sign of the vagrant; and slovenly speech, of the cultured bum.

Some people swear because they lack the ability and the vocabulary to express exactly how they really feel. They have a few profane expressions, like blank checks, that you can fill in with whatever you want. Everything is either damn sad or damn funny, hot as Hell or cold as Hell. Oliver Wendell Holmes was referring to these persons when he wrote: "I have known several genteel idiots whose whole vocabulary had deliquesced into some half dozen expressions" *(The Autocrat of the Breakfast Table,* pp. 202-203).

Often profanity results from bad company and thoughtlessness. Beware of falling into the habit of profanity. The first time you may or may not choose to do it. If you do it, the second time you will do it because you choose it. And the third time you will do it whether you choose to or not.

Finally, profanity is a sign of a lack of faith and good manners. You can generally tell the country a stranger is from by the language he speaks. So we can tell what country will be ours by the language we speak. The language of Heaven is that of praise and glory to God; the language of Hell is profanity and cursing. Which is our country?

Some "satirist" listed ten reasons why I swear:
1. It pleases my mother and father.
2. It is a mark of my manliness.
3. It proves I have self-control.
4. It makes my conversation pleasing to everybody.
5. It impresses people that I have more than an ordinary education.
6. It leaves no doubt about my good breeding.
7. It is a sign of my culture and refinement.
8. It makes me desirable company for women and children.
9. It shows what a wonderful vocabulary I have.
10. It is my way of honoring God.

It is good to have a safety-valve: expressions that are emphatic, but not sinful. For instance, "You parallelepiped"; "Confound it"; "By ginger!" When I was teaching English, I used to say to the students when they could not get a point, "You blocks, you stones, you worse than senseless things." Later on, they discovered the expression was from Shakespeare. That is constructive emphatic language.

One golfer used to exclaim when he missed a putt, "Oh, Grand Coulee!" Someone asked him what kind of an expression was that. He answered, "It's the biggest dam on earth."

One day while a girl was in church, the janitor was cleaning it. Jesus said to the girl, *"See that man. He's cleaning up my house. Tell people to clean up their mouths, to speak in love, with respect, and with reverence. If they honor me, they must honor my name, for it stands for me."*

God calls each one of us by name (*Isaiah* 43:1). For He respects us, and the name is the icon of the person (cp., *Sirach* 23:9).

Whenever we hear the name of Jesus used profanely, make reparation by saying, "Blessed be the name of Jesus!"

Chapter 6

Why is it wrong to miss Mass deliberately on Sunday?

There are many reasons why it is wrong to miss Sunday Mass deliberately.

First of all, to miss Mass deliberately on Sunday after Sunday leads to a loss of faith—the greatest of all tragedies. In his *Life of Milton*, Samuel Johnson summed up what it means to miss weekly worship in two sentences: "To be of no church is dangerous. Religion, of which is animated by faith and hope, will glide by degrees out of the mind, unless it be invigorated and reimpressed by external ordinances by stated calls to worship."

Our Lord expressly recommended common prayer . . . and promised that whenever two or three were gathered together in His name He would be there in the midst of them (*Matthew* 18:20).

When we pray together, our minds are normally far more alert than when we pray alone.

Public prayer is far more powerful than private prayer to appease the anger of God and draw down His mercy. That is why the Church in times of public calamity asks for public prayers.

When people pray together, it is far more formidable to the devil than when praying alone, because public prayer is an army that is attacking him. Soldiers join together in an army to overcome an enemy. In a tug of war, many join others to overcome the opposition. It is very easy to break a single stick; but if you join it to a bundle of other sticks, you won't be able to break it. A single strand of hemp can easily be broken; but intertwine it with many other strands and you make an unbreakable rope.

Moreover, participation in Sunday Mass is a testimony that one is a Catholic. It is a witness one belongs to the Church. It is a testimony to God's holiness and a hope of salvation.

Furthermore, attendance at Sunday Mass provides a support community for others (*Heb.* 10:25). The Mass is not like going to a movie, where people can enjoy themselves and never look at anyone else. Nor is it like a cafeteria, where everyone can pick and choose what he or she likes, regardless of everyone else. No, the Mass is, like the Last Supper, a gathering of friends, of people who care for each other. At this table we are fed by the Word of the Lord and His Body and Blood. This outpouring of grace, plus the example of all the others present, empowers us to go out into the world and be and do what we are supposed to be and to do.

Finally, we ought to go to Sunday Mass to pay our bills. We "owe" God, remember? We owe God for our life. We depend on Him for life, more than the electric bulb depends on the current of electricity, more than the sunbeam depends on the sun, more than the baby in its mother's womb depends on its mother. If it is wrong to refuse to pay what you owe the baker for the bread with which you nourish your life, how much more wrong is it to refuse to pay what you owe God for the life which that bread nourishes. Sunday Mass is simply our way of thanking God our Father for loving us so much.

Sunday Mass is rooted in a practice that goes back to the time of the Lord and His apostles. It is there in *Luke* 24:30; *Acts* 20:7; *Heb.* 10:25; and through numerous letters and documents of the early Church—such as the *Letter of St.*

Ignatius to the Magnesians (#9). It is part of the documents of Vatican II: *Constitution on the Sacred Liturgy,* #106.

About the year A.D. 150, St. Justin Martyr wrote in his *Defense of Christianity:* "On the day which is called after the sun, all those who live in the city or in the country come together . . . they read Holy Scripture, pray for general intentions, bring sacrificial gifts of bread and wine; and then in a solemn prayer of thanksgiving the gifts are no longer bread and wine but become the Body and Blood of Christ, of which all present receive. Portions are carried even to those who were absent." Such was the Sunday celebration in the second century.

In those days assemblies of this kind involved great danger. Yet Christians risked their lives because Jesus had commanded them to do this in memory of Himself. They realized that the memory of Christ and His deeds was the basis for Christian living and Christian civilization.

The Council of Elvira (c. A.D. 300), the Council of Laodicea (c. A.D. 390) and the Apostolic Constitutions (also about A.D. 390) called for assistance at Mass and cessation from work on Sundays.

In keeping with this ancient tradition, the Code of Canon Law says: "On Sundays and other holy days of obligation the faithful **are bound** to participate in the Mass" (*Canon* 1247). Are bound—no ifs or ands!

Thus the *Catechism of the Catholic Church (CCC)* writes: "Those who deliberately fail in this obligation commit a grave sin" (*CCC,* #2181).

Parodying the time-worn excuses people give for not attending Sunday Mass, a pastor wrote this satirical piece called, "Reasons Why I Never Wash":
1. I was made to wash as a child.
2. People who wash are hypocrites . . . they think they are cleaner than other people.

3. There are so many different kinds of soap, I could never decide which one was right.
4. I used to wash, but it got so boring so I stopped.
5. I still wash on special days, like Christmas and Easter.
6. None of my friends wash.
7. I'm young—when I'm older and dirtier, I might wash.
8. People who make soap are only after your money.

Chapter 7

Why is it wrong to do unnecessary work on Sunday?

The Jewish *Talmud* devotes two complete books to the Sabbath. It asks: "How is the Sabbath to be observed?" And then answers: "With prayer and study, with good food and drink, with clean and becoming clothes, with rest and joy."

Among the Jews this observance must have been ancient, for Moses begins this commandment with "Remember"; that is, don't forget to keep this time-honored custom. *"Remember to keep holy the Lord's day."*

The word "holy" means "different" or "separate" or "set apart." One day in the week is to be kept different from the others. It is to be a special day, when we remember that the Lord is our God, and so a day of worship and a day of rest.

The Christian Sunday continues the tradition of having one special day each week. It was changed from Saturday to Sunday, because on Sunday Jesus rose from the dead. But it keeps the two marks of the Jewish Sabbath: worship and rest.

We celebrate the Resurrection especially by the Eucharist, which is a thanksgiving for this astounding fact.

The other side of the celebration is to make Sunday a day of rest. The *Catechism* says: "On Sundays and other holy days of obligation, the faithful are to refrain from engaging in work or activities that hinder the **worship** owed to God, the **joy** proper to the Lord's Day, the performance of the **works of mercy**, and the appropriate **relaxation** of mind and body" (*CCC*, #2184-5).

The Church retained the old Jewish ban on Sunday work to safeguard freedom and to protect working people from the greed of their employers.

First, a person should be free from work once a week. Periodic rest and refreshment are a physical necessity (*Exodus* 23:12). *"God knows how we are formed"* (*Ps.* 103:14). All work and no play not only makes Jack a dull boy, but even his father and mother. In World War II, a seven-day work-week was introduced under the pressure of war. What happened? Industry became plagued with absenteeism. Machines need rest; and people are not machines.

Secondly, people should be protected against the greed of employers. The greed of employers and the dictates of market competition are posing an unnecessary threat to the special character that distinguishes Sunday from the workdays, and are making unreasonable demands upon workers.

One of the most terrible concessions today to secularism and greed is Sunday shopping. There is absolutely no excuse for food markets, and other businesses, to stay open on Sundays. Families decades ago got along without Sunday shopping, and that was in an age when there were no refrigerators, freezers, quick transportation, or five-day week.

Business magazines tell us that Sunday opening rarely increases the total volume of business; it just spreads over seven days what could be done in six. Nobody gains; everybody loses.

We should not sacrifice our Sundays at the altars of cellophane and cash registers. We should not permit a small, selfish, grasping minority to eliminate the Sunday rest. There is no need, but greed. Public authority should protect our traditions from unbridled economic forces.

Furthermore, workers should have a **common day** of rest. If a worker's free day comes in the middle of the week when everybody else is working, he cannot really enjoy his freedom. A variable work week makes it impossible to do things together, with others, and thus get proper rest, relaxation, and joy. Again, industry is responsible to see that this indirect attack on the Sunday does not happen.

What ought we to do on Sundays?

It is not enough just to go to Sunday Mass and to rest. A danger here is that the day of rest can easily become a day of restlessness. If it does, people will drift into doing weekday chores just to fill up the void.

Therefore, don't focus on the negative side, avoiding unnecessary work; rather, focus on the Church's total vision of Sunday.

On Sundays, break your weekday patterns. Get up late if you will. Have a lavish breakfast. Visit friends. Don't worry about anything. Just enjoy the day. Whatever you do, do leisurely, quietly, and joyfully without rush, fuss, or any utilitarian motive.

Do works of mercy: visit the sick, the infirm, and the elderly.

Devote time to the family and relatives. Bring back the Sunday dinner, where all get together to enjoy not only eating together, but sharing together. Dress up in your best instead of casually wearing your ordinary weekday clothes.

Take time to reflect and cultivate mind and soul, by good reading and meditation. Pray in a different way at a different time, for instance, the family Rosary.

Avoid unnecessary work. Necessary work, like that of doctors, nurses, police officers, and fire fighters, is one thing. But unnecessary work—mowing the lawn, painting the house, redecorating the rec room—is not in keeping with the spirit of the Sunday rest.

In this way you will be imitating God, who on the seventh day, took a long, loving look at the world and delighted in it. We too must take time to smell the roses and thus share in God's delight.

"This is the day the Lord has made. Let us be glad and rejoice in it" (*Ps.* 118:24).

Chapter 8

Why must we love, honor, and obey our parents?

Next to God, those most deserving of honor and love are our parents; for next to God, no one else is more responsible for our life and knowledge of God than our parents. God creates; parents procreate.

Parents so intimately cooperate with God in bringing life into the world and in bringing it up in the world that the commandment to honor our parents heads the second table of the Ten Commandments dealing with our neighbor, just as those pertaining to God heads the first table. Like the third commandment, regarding keeping holy the Lord's day, this commandment is also couched in positive terms, and not in the negative terms of "Thou shalt not . . . ."

God made us to image Himself. God is a Trinity: a community of loving Persons. So God meant for us to live in community. That is why He gave us the gift of speech and language: so that we might be able to communicate with others and build up society. For the same end, God made mankind, male and female. He gave the first woman to the first man that the two might become one as God is one. And He told them to increase and multiply that they might become many persons. In other words, the very first society that God created was the family.

The family is the oldest institution in the world, established by God Himself in the Garden of Eden. It preexists both Church and State, which exist, among other reasons, to support and strengthen marriage and the family. The

Catechism of the Catholic Church lists some of the rights of families that the State should protect:

- the right to have a family and adequate means to support it;
- the right to bring up children in accordance with the family's own traditions and religious and cultural values;
- the right to housing suitable for proper family life. . .

and so on (*CCC*, #2211);

Now for men and women to live harmoniously and productively in society, there has to be someone in charge, in authority. So God put the man and woman who form the family, the parents, in charge of the family. He said: *"Honor your father and your mother"* (*Ex.* 20:12).

Children are to do this by loving, honoring, and obeying their parents.

Children should **love** their parents, for parents give life and love to them (*Sir.* 7:27-28).

Children should **honor** their parents, for their parents take the place of God. Children must give them material and moral support in old age, illness, loneliness and distress (*Sir.* 3:2-6).

Alexander the Great so honored his mother Olympia that when one of his leaders criticized her, Alexander burst out: "Doesn't the fool know that all his arguments avail nothing against one tear of my mother?"

When Coriolanus besieged Rome, his friends and all the officers of the city came out pleading with him not to destroy Rome. But to no avail. But when his mother Volumnia came out and pleaded with her son, she did what all the swords in Italy and her confederate arms could not do—she saved Rome, so greatly did Coriolanus honor her.

St. Thomas More was noted for the great respect that he always showed his father.

As children treat their parents, so shall they in turn be treated by their own children. Jacob lied to Isaac; his children lied to him about Joseph (*Gn.* 27:19; 37:32).

"The eye that mocks a father, or scorns an aged mother, will be plucked out by the ravens in the valley; the young eagles will devour it" (*Proverbs* 30:17).

The great sign of honor is **obedience**. Children must love and honor their parents all days even after their death; they must obey them until legal maturity and in all that is not sinful. Regarding one's vocation in life, choosing a spouse or the religious life, children should consult their parents, and parents may advise and guide them, but not command them.

The model for obedience to parents is Jesus Himself. The Scripture says, *"He was obedient to them"*—to Joseph and to Mary—(*Luke* 2:51).

Jesus roundly condemned the scribes and the Pharisees for using their man-made traditions to set aside the honor and love due to parents (*Mark* 7:8-13).

In his letter to the Ephesians, St. Paul wrote: *"Children, obey your parents . . ."*; then he added the observation that this was the only commandment to which a promise of long life had been added (*Eph.* 6:1-3; *Sirach* 3:6).

"Honor your father and your mother, that you may have a long life in the land which the Lord, your God is giving you" (*Ex.* 20:12).

The Christian family should image the Trinity. The father must be love—a provider and protector, like God the Father. The mother must radiate love in the family, like God the Holy Spirit in the Trinity. And the children should reflect the obedience of the Son of God to Mary and Joseph.

The Christian family constitutes **a domestic church**, for it is a place where faith, prayer, and love should bind its members together. A strong family leads to a healthy society and a vigorous nation; and a holy family leads to a prosperous local and universal Church.

Chapter 9

Why is it wrong to take the life
of another on my own authority?

Basically, to take the life of another on our own authority is wrong for the simple reason that life is not ours to take. God is the author of life. The Psalmist said: *"The Lord's are the earth and its fullness: the world and those who dwell in it"* (*Ps.* 24:1). If I build a house, it is mine, and you have no right to sell it or burn it down. Life belongs to God; and it is His. We are stewards of our life; He has rented it to us for one single purpose: that we may use it to gain eternal life with Himself.

Thus when Cain murdered his brother Abel, God deplored the act and denounced Cain.

When Noah stepped out of the ark after the Flood, God issued a command against murder: *"If anyone sheds the blood of man, by man shall his blood be shed; for in the image of God has man been made* (*Genesis* 9:6). So in the Old Testament blood was a sacred sign of life. To shed it in murder was to sin against the holiness of God, the giver of life, and against the dignity of man. It is the sign of the beast.

So God specifically prohibited killing: *"The innocent and the just you shall not put to death"* (*Exodus* 23:7). And this law obliges everyone, everywhere, and at all times.

To take one's own life is suicide. Again we have no right to take what is not ours. Shakespeare in *Hamlet* wrote: "The Everlasting hath fixed His canon against self-slaughter."

Napoleon called suicide "an act of cowardice."

Of course valor is not suicide. Colin P. Kelly, in World War II (December 22, 1941), gave his life to save the lives of his comrades. He didn't want to destroy his life; he wanted to save his comrades. But in doing this, he lost his life. We call this the Principal of Double Effect: one good and one bad; the good is willed, the bad foreseen but not willed; and the good and bad effects happen together; and the good effect outweighs the evil.

Also, to take the life of another on one's own authority is murder, such as the crimes of infanticide, fratricide, parricide, and the murder of one's own spouse (*CCC*, #2268).

However, legitimate defense of persons and societies is not an exception to the prohibition against murder of the innocent that constitutes intentional killing. A person has a right to defend himself against an unjust aggressor. If in so doing, he slays the other, he is not guilty of murder.

The act of self-defense falls under the Principle of Double Effect: the preservation of one's own life, and the killing of the aggressor. The one is intended, the other is not.

Legitimate self-defense is not only a right for individuals, but it is also a right and a grave duty for those responsible for the common good of the family or of the State.

If the aggressor is a person, the State can inflict the punishment of death in cases of extreme gravity (*CCC*, #2266).

About the death penalty, the Holy Father said in his encyclical *The Gospel of Life* (*GOL*, March 25, 1995) that it is not to be used "except in cases of absolute necessity: in other words, when it would not be possible otherwise to defend society. Today, however, as a result of steady improvements in the organization of the penal system, such cases are very rare, if not practically not-existent" (*GOL*, #56).

The phrases "very rare" and "practically non-existent" do

not mean that the death penalty is wrong, but only that it should be used very rarely. The term "very rare" is a relative one: does it mean seldom, few, occasional—one execution out of 200 murders, or 500 executions in the circumstances of 20,000 murders? The terms "very rare" and "practically non-existent" are far too indefinite to establish a moral and doctrinal certainty. In other words, no one can say it is un-Catholic or disobedient to the Pope to approve of execution.

The primary effect of punishment is:
- to redress the disorder caused by the offense;
- to preserve public order and the safety of persons;
- to act as a deterrent;
- to contribute to the correction of the offender—when punishment is voluntarily accepted by the offender, it takes on the value of expiation (*CCC*, #2266).

Finally, if the aggressors be armed forces, those in authority have a right to repel these forces, by war if necessary. The conditions for legitimate defense by military force require rigorous considerations:

- the damage inflicted by the aggressor on the nation or community of nations must be lasting, grave and certain;
- all other means of putting an end to it must have been shown to be impractical or ineffective;
- there must be serious prospects of success;
- the use of arms must not produce evils and disorders graver than the evil to be eliminated (*CCC*, #2309).

Citizens are obliged to fight for their country.

Conscientious objectors must be respected, but they must serve their country in some other way.

Even in war, the moral law must be observed; therefore, non-combatants, the wounded, or prisoners, must be treated humanly and with respect.

Genocide is a mortal sin.

The arms race does not ensure peace.

When injustice, excessive social and economic inequalities, envy, distrust, and pride prevail, there will always be unrest. But when glory is given to God in the highest, then there will be peace on earth among men.

Chapter 10

Why are abortion and euthanasia wrong?

One of the great travesties of humanity is to advocate the destruction of life at its beginning (abortion) and at its end (euthanasia), under the pretext of achieving some greater good. Our culture of death tries to interpret the crimes of abortion and euthanasia as legitimate expressions of individual freedom, to be acknowledged and protected as actual rights.

Pope John Paul II said: "Man's life comes from God; it is His gift, His image and imprint, a sharing in His breath of life. God therefore is the sole Lord of this life; man cannot do with it as he wills. God himself makes this clear to Noah after the Flood: *'From man in regard to his fellow man I will demand an accounting for human life'* " (*Genesis* 9:5)—(*GOL*, #39).

Verbal engineering goes before social change, so those who defend abortion call the unborn baby in its mother's womb a "fetus" and not a human being. The dogma of the Immaculate Conception rejects this argument. The dogma teaches that Mary, from the very first instance of her **conception**, was free from sin and filled with God's grace. But sin and grace attach only to a person. So Mary from the first instance of her conception was a person; and so is every other unborn child.

The Church says: "From the time that the ovum is fertilized, a life is begun which is neither that of the father nor the mother; it is rather the life of a new human being with his own growth. It would never be made human if it were

not human already. Modern genetics now confirms this"
(*GOL*, #60). A bird is a bird whether in the nest or outside
the nest. A child is a child in the womb or outside it. "Place"
in philosophy is only an accident.

That is why the Church from the very beginning always
condemned abortion: it is the murder of an innocent, defense-
less child. So said the Didache (A.D. 70-90); so said the
Epistle attributed to Barnabas (A.D. 96-98); so said Vatican
II, which termed abortion an "unspeakable crime" (*Pastoral
Constitution on the Church in the Modern World*, #51).

To underscore the gravity of this offense, the Church has
attached to the act automatic excommunication (*Canon*,
1398). The excommunication affects all those who commit
this crime and all those accomplices without whose help the
crime would not have been committed. The purpose of the
penalty is not only to make known the gravity of the sin but
also to foster conversion and repentance.

Besides this abominable crime of abortion, there is the
tragedy of euthanasia. Euthanasia is an action or omission
which of itself and by intention causes death, with the purpose of eliminating suffering (*GOL*, #65). Euthanasia
means taking control of death and bringing it about before
its time to end suffering. It is both senseless and inhumane.

Our present day culture has lost the sense of the value of
suffering. God in His mercy permits sufferings at the end of
life because, suffering, when freely accepted, can shorten or
eliminate Purgatory. St. Catherine of Siena said sin is like
owing God a million dollars. We can pay the million dollars
now with a penny; if we don't, then, later on, we'll have to
pay the million in Purgatory. For a tiny act of suffering
freely accepted here on earth is worth more than the most
terrible sufferings hereafter. The reason is we have free will
now; after death the night comes when no man can work.

Remember these facts:

- Jesus' greatest work came at the end of His life, when enduring unspeakable sufferings. His sufferings were redemptive; so can ours be if accepted freely as Jesus did His—"through the bitter paths to the stars."
- If a disease is incurable and painful, patient acceptance will merit great rewards in the life to come. St. Paul gloried in the cross, for he said: *"I consider that the sufferings of this present time are as nothing compared with the glory to be revealed for us"* (*Romans* 8:18).
- Moreover God will always give the grace to bear any trial— *"My grace is sufficient for you"* (*2 Cor.* 12:9).
- If a person is disabled, others are given the opportunity to practice charity and compassion and to thank God for having protected them from similar crosses. Thus Shakespeare said: "Sweet are the uses of adversity."
- If euthanasia were legal, then what incentive would there be for research? Fear would haunt the aged.

The Greek physician Hippocrates (+357 B.C.) in his famous oath said: "I will give no deadly medicine to anyone if asked, nor suggest any such counsel." He was a pagan; we're supposed to be Christians!

One of the specific characteristics of the present-day attacks on human life consists in the trend to demand a legal justification for them, as if they were rights which the State must acknowledge as belonging to citizens.

"Such a culture of death, taken as a whole, betrays a completely individualistic concept of freedom, which ends up by becoming the freedom of the 'strong' against the weak who have no choice but to submit" (*GOL*, #19).

The basis of these tendencies is Ethical Relativism: the will of the majority, a Gallup Poll morality. Democracy is being substituted for morality. Democracy is a form of government; it is not the norm of morality. Governments are not above the moral law. "There is a law," William Seward said, "higher than the Constitution"—the Law of God. Civil law must be based on the moral law. It must aim to defend the common good by protecting the rights of all citizens, including the unborn and the aged. This is so, because:

- People pre-existed the State. The State exists for the people, not the people for the State.
- People are nobler in nature than the State. They image God and have an eternal destiny; whereas the State images man and has only a temporal destiny.
- People—because they have immortal souls—are endowed by God with certain unalienable Rights, "that among these are Life, Liberty, and the Pursuit of Happiness—That to secure these Rights, Governments are instituted."

"In the case of an intrinsically unjust law, such as a law permitting abortion or euthanasia, it is therefore never licit to obey it, or to 'take part in a propaganda campaign in favor of such a law, or vote for it' " (*GOL*, #73).

We are a people of life and for life. *"I came so that they may have life and have it more abundantly"* (*John* 10:10).

Note regarding extraordinary means for prolonging life: "Discontinuing medical procedures that are burdensome, dangerous, extraordinary, or disproportionate to the expected outcome can be legitimate . . . . Here one does not will to cause death; one's inability to impede it is merely accepted" (*CCC,* #2278).

Chapter 11

Why is it wrong to commit adultery?

The two most basic instincts of man are—self-preservation and preservation of the race.

To preserve self, we eat and we drink. To preserve the race, we marry. To get us to eat and drink and to marry, God has attached an intense pleasure to these actions. The pleasure attached to the married act surpasses that attached to eating and drinking, for the preservation of the race is more necessary than the preservation of an individual.

Pleasure, therefore, is simply bait, a lure, a "come-on," to get us to do something very important for ourselves and for the race. **Pleasure is not an end in itself!** It is God's way of getting us to do something very important and His way of saying, "Thank you," for doing it. The pleasure in eating and drinking is God's way to get us to eat and to drink and His way of thanking us for saving our life. The pleasure accompanying the married act is God's way of getting us to save the race and His thank you for doing just that.

However to seek the pleasure only without reference to the purpose of the action is to do something wrong. Were we to eat only for the pleasure of it and gormandize ourselves, we would be guilty of gluttony. Were we to drink only for pleasure of it and become drunkards, we would again be doing something very wrong.

The same is true of sex. Just to have sex for the pleasure, or as some teenagers say, "just for the fun of it," without any reference to bringing life into the world and bringing it up in the world, is also terribly wrong. And this is even worse when one's sex partner is married to somebody else. Such an action is adultery.

To illustrate what I mean, take the eyes for example. If I were to ask you, "What is the purpose of the eyes?" I am sure everyone of you could tell me in a jiffy. You would say the purpose of the eyes is to see. And you wouldn't need the Catholic Church to tell you. You would say that because that's what the eyes do.

Now the eyes are beautiful. To enhance their beauty, some women use mascara, false eyelashes, eye shadow, and so on. Nothing wrong with that. A thing of beauty is a joy forever. But just suppose, suppose that the makeup was causing blindness. Would you use it? You wouldn't. And why? Because vision, not beauty, is the purpose of the eyes.

The same is true of sex. Sex is beautiful. But the purpose of married sex is life. How do we know? Well, the sex act normally ends in life. That is the normal way life comes into the world. Sex is so geared toward life that there are no foolproof artificial contraceptives. The only way to prevent life coming from the sex act is to mutilate the human body by a tubal ligation or vasectomy. What's that telling us? Isn't that telling us that God meant sex to be the gateway of life?

To use it solely for pleasure and to block the entrance of life into the world is to pervert the action and its purpose, and to do something as equally bad, or worse, as gluttony, drunkenness, or sacrificing vision for beauty.

Chastity is simply the virtue that inclines a person to go along with God's purpose regarding sex. It chastises the passions; it curbs them so that they will not run wild.

Sex is a good thing; it enables us to share in God's creation. Hence it is sacred as life itself. But it must be used in the context of marriage, a sacred contract between two to be faithful to each other till death.

Chastity is simply having the guts to use sex according to

reason or God's plan. **Outside of marriage**, it expresses itself in purity: avoiding all sex acts that could lead to intercourse, such as passionate kissing, petting, etc. **Within marriage**, it means being exclusive (no third party), opened to life (no contraception or abortifacients), and till death (no divorce).

Chastity frees you from pregnancy, a hurry-up wedding, abortion decision, guilt, sexually transmitted diseases, being used, loss of reputation, ruining your future—as candy before dinner can spoil the dinner.

To be chaste, remember that our bodies are temples of the Holy Spirit; therefore they deserve the highest reverence (*1 Cor.* 6:12-20).

St. Paul warned that *"bad company corrupts good morals"* (*1 Cor.* 15:33). Sirach wrote: *"He who touches pitch blackens his hand"* (13:1). Therefore, avoid all occasions of sin: bad companions, pornographic magazines and books, too much television, some hard rock music.

Alessandro Serenelli, who stabbed St. Maria Goretti to death because she would not commit sex sins with him, confessed that bad magazines made him do what he did.

Lorenzo Scupoli in his classic book, *The Spiritual Combat*, always counsels us to fight temptation head on; the only time he advises us to retreat is when we are being tempted against purity. He writes: "Fly from the occasions of sin, for thou art as stubble." The strongest steel will melt in fire, so will all good resolutions in the heat of passion. So the best fight against impurity is flight!

Above all, go to monthly Confession, frequent Holy Communion, pray the Rosary daily, and read the lives of the saints.

Chapter 12

Why the sexes? Why sex?

To answer these two questions, we must go back to the story of creation, the first two chapters of *Genesis*.

After God had made the world a fit place to dwell in, God said, *"Let us make man in Our image, after Our likeness. So God created man in His image; in the divine image He created him"* (*Genesis* 1:26-27).

Three times, God says He made man to image Himself. To image God is to reflect two things about God: **What** He is and **Who** He is.

What is God? God is love (*1 John* 4:16). Love is a relational quality, a relationship between two. You cannot love unless there is another one to be loved, just as you cannot clap with one hand. It takes two to tango, two to tangle, and two to love. So God said: *"It is not good for the man to be alone"* (*Genesis* 2:18). Alone, man could not love. So God created the sexes: He made male and female (*Genesis* 1:27).

So, why the sexes? God created the sexes so that man could love like God and thus image what God is.

Now, who is God? God is a Trinity; that is, one God in three divine Persons. In other words, God is one and at the same time He is many. God is a community of loving Persons.

So why sex? To image this **oneness** and this **manyness** of God.

To reflect the oneness of God, God made sex **UNI-**

TIVE: able to unite two and make them one. Love gives; and married love gives itself to have and to hold till death. Thus when God celebrated the first marriage, He said, *"That is why a man leaves his father and mother and clings to his wife, and the two of them become one"* (*Genesis* 2:24; *Mt.* 19:4).

To reflect the many Persons in the Trinity, God made sex **PROCREATIVE**: the gateway of life. Thus God commanded the first man and woman: *"Be fertile and multiply"* (*Genesis* 1:28); that is, create a community of persons, a family. A family is one in name and many in members, thus it images the one God of many Persons. The father of the family is meant to reflect God the Father in providing and protecting the family. The Mother is to reflect God the Holy Spirit by radiating love within the home. And the children are to reflect God the Son by their obedience to their parents. Thus Abp. Fulton J. Sheen defined sex as "the capacity to procreate given to man to image the triune God."

Because God made sex to express a love that is both unitive and procreative, sex can be used only in the context of married love. For only in marriage is love **unitive**, making two persons one; **procreative**, bringing life into the world; and **till death**, being able to parent that life. Only in such a context can God's purpose for sex be fulfilled.

As a word must be the expression of an idea, so sex must be the expression of a love that is exclusive till death and always open to life.

The words of an insane person can be meaningless, because they are not the expression of a sane mind; so sex, when not the expression of a love that is exclusive, till death, and always open to life, can be a tragic fraud, a lie, a meaningless act.

The connection between the unitive and procreative aspects of sex is inseparable and willed by God and unable to be broken by man on his own initiative (*Humanae Vitae*, #12).

Any person who tries to separate these two elements contradicts the will of God, acts contrary to it, and therefore does what is intrinsically immoral. For *"what God has joined together, no human being must separate"* (*Matt.* 19:6).

Starting with this principle, established by God Himself, namely that sex must always be the expression of a love that is unitive, procreative, and till death, we can arrive at a simple Sexual Ethics Primer. We can state:

1. Masturbation is wrong, because it is neither unitive nor procreative. No life, no life-giving possible. Just self-gratification. Dead end street!
2. Pre-marital sex is always wrong, because the union is not unitive till death. Gratification usually replaces commitment and sacrifice.
3. Condoms, as well as the pill, artificial contraceptives, and abortifacients are wrong for single persons, because the union is neither till death nor open to life; and for married persons, because the union is not procreative or open to life.
4. Homosexual acts and lesbian acts are acts of grave depravity, for though sometimes unitive, they are not procreative. Such acts have no biological purpose, no life, no future; their sole aim is self-gratification.

    For those afflicted with a homosexual inclination, it can be a trial. We must be kind, compassionate and sensitive to such persons, and try to help them to be chaste. But in no way can we condone homosexual acts (*CCC*, #2257-2259).

5. Abortion is a horrendous crime: it is taking an innocent, defenseless, human life. It does not solve
   teenage pregnancy.

Ten little words will solve the AIDS crisis:
   ABSTINENCE BEFORE MARRIAGE;
   FIDELITY AFTER MARRIAGE; and
   NO INTRAVENOUS ILLEGAL DRUGS.

Chapter 13

Why is it wrong to covet your neighbor's wife?

First of all, we must understand what "covet" means. To covet means to want someone or something wrongfully or unlawfully. To want to be a saint is not coveting. That's a good desire or emulation. We ought to emulate the saints and our heroes: to want to be like them. That's good. But coveting is a **bad** desire, like David coveting Uriah's wife, or Ahab coveting the vineyard of Naboth.

Why is coveting wrong? It is wrong because desire leads to action. As you think so you act. Bad desires and bad thoughts will very likely lead to bad actions. Covetousness is simply bad desires and bad thoughts. See what coveting did to David and Ahab. David had Uriah killed to get his wife (*2 Samuel* 11). Jezebal had Naboth killed so her husband Ahab could get his vineyard (*1 Kings* 21).

Jesus branded the Pharisees a *"brood of vipers,"* because they had bad hearts; and, because they had, Jesus went on to say, *"How can you say good things when you are evil? For from the fullness of the heart the mouth speaks"* (*Matt.* 12:34). And on another occasion, *"from the heart comes evil thoughts, murder, adultery, unchastity . . ."* (*Matt..* 15:19).

So, in His sermon on the Mount, Jesus warned against covetous thoughts: *"You have heard that it was said, 'You shall not commit adultery.' But I say to you, everyone who looks at a woman with lust has already committed adultery with her in his heart"* (*Matt.* 5:28).

So the ninth commandment forbids in thought and desire

what the sixth commandment forbids in act.

Impure thoughts and desires arise in our minds and hearts like weeds in a garden. Generally, in the beginning they are temptations. There are four steps to a temptation: first, there is the **sensation**, then the **reaction**, then the **realization**, and finally the **decision**.

Suppose a mother is taking her child through the toy department of a large department store before Christmas. Her child sees a toy he wants (the sensation). He tugs at his mother's dress, stops her, points to the toy, and says, "Mommy I want that toy" (the reaction). The mother looks at the toy, considers the price, knows her own pocketbook (the realization). Then she decides whether or not to get the toy for him (the decision). Up to the time of the decision, all the actions are a temptation.

The same pattern is true of impure thoughts or desires. Generally, they are generated by perhaps a suggestive picture or a pornographic magazine (the sensation). The reaction is immediate—one feels drawn to dwell upon the thought or desire (the reaction). Then reason, illuminated by grace, says, "Wait a minute. Turn away from looking at that picture. Stop reading that magazine" (the realization). Up to that point, all is temptation. Then comes the important step: your decision.

You can decide to do one of three things: to take your eyes off the picture or set the magazine aside (an act of virtue); or you can dilly-dally, you can play with fire: take one more look or read one more page (a venial sin of imprudence); or you can give a deaf ear to grace and give in totally to the temptation, even allowing yourself to indulge in an impure action (a mortal sin).

Remember the feelings of step two (the reaction) are not a sin—no matter how strong they may be. Feelings are not moral. Feeling good doesn't make you good; feeling bad doesn't make you bad. St. Francis de Sales says, *"Sentire non est peccatum, sed consentire"*—"To feel is not the sin, but to consent."

St. Catherine of Siena had a terrible temptation to impurity. After the storm had passed, she complained, "Where were you, Lord, when my spirit was shaken by the spasm of temptation?" God answered, *"Catherine, I was deep in your heart, taking delight in your resistance and strengthening you in the struggle."*

Temptations are a good sign. St. Francis de Sales wrote: "It is a very good sign if our enemy knocks and storms at the door, for it shows he is not where he wishes to be" (De Sales, *Consoling Thoughts*, p. 154).

God permits temptations, because temptations can strengthen us. *"Whom the Lord loves, he disciplines"* (*Heb.* 12:6).

Opposing winds cause the kite to fly high in the sky. The winds of temptation can cause us to fly high to God for help to fight them.

The mountain stream fighting its way down the mountainside sparkles. Stagnant at the foot of the mountain, it becomes polluted and putrid. Idle iron rusts.

Consider weeds and roses; they are both plants, both are nurtured by the same soil and sun. Our thoughts and desires are like weeds and roses. Bad thoughts and bad desires, the weeds; good thoughts and good desires, the roses. The choice is ours: weedy thoughts and desires or rosy ones. We can dwell in unloveliness and unfruitfulness or we can dwell with joy and achievement. We can make our minds and hearts a weed patch or a flower garden. We are the gardeners.

"Blessed are the clean of heart, for they will see God" (*Matt.* 5:8).

Chapter 14

Why is it wrong to steal?

Why can't I steal? The reason is simple: I have no right to take what belongs to another against his reasonable will. The presumption here is that I have a right to own, to say that this belongs to me and not to you.

There are two reasons why I have a right to own.

One is because I have a right to provide for my future: for old age, sickness, children. But this cannot be done without the right to own.

The more basic reason, however, why I have a right to own is that I have a right to life. This right to life is given to each one of us by God Himself. The Declaration of Independence says, "We are endowed **by our Creator** with certain unalienable Rights, that among these are **Life**, Liberty and the Pursuit of Happiness."

God, not man, not the State, gives us life.

But God also gives us all that we need to sustain that life. That is why God created the world before He created man—so that man could get the food, the clothing, the shelter he needed to keep alive.

Therefore, man has a God-given right to food, clothing, and shelter. But in using food, clothing, and shelter, man destroys them. Therefore, man has a right to destroy the food he eats, the clothing he wears, and the shelter he uses.

The right to use a thing with the power to destroy is what we mean by **ownership**. Therefore, each one of us has a God-given right to own; to call something our own; to say, "It's mine." What is mine is not yours. You have no right to take what is mine against my reasonable will.

I say "against my reasonable will," because our right to own is not absolute, but relative to our neighbor's needs. We might draw three circles around ourselves. In the circle closest to us are all the things that are **absolutely necessary** for life, like food, clothing, and shelter. In the next circle are all the things that are **relatively necessary**; that is, necessary for us to live according to our station in life. In the outer circle are the **unnecessary, superfluous things**, like luxuries, for instance, a yacht.

Our right becomes stronger the more necessary the thing is for life. If a man were starving and had exhausted all other legitimate means for acquiring food, he would have the right to take from his neighbor, who had plenty, that which was necessary to preserve his life. He would have a right to do that.

A final important thought on this matter: **our right to own imposes responsibility on the owners**, for the right is personal, but the use is social. In capitalism, the owners are the stockholders, but they do not shoulder the responsibility for running the industry. Therefore, should they take all the profits? *Sirach* warns: *"For the sake of profit, many sin, and the struggle for wealth blinds the eyes"* (27:1).

One idea to change this would be an industrial democracy in the capitalistic system; that is:

- Employees could be given a share in the profits over and above the just wage, for they helped make it.
- They could be given the right to share in management, by being given representation on the Board of Directors.
- Finally, they could be given a share in the ownership through annual bonuses of stocks.

Industrial democracy is not only just, but it would make the worker more interested than ever in the industry.

Our right to own is protected **from the inside** by the virtue of justice. Justice is a virtue that inclines us to give to another what is his due, to respect the rights of others, especially their God-given right to own.

Our right to own is protected **from the outside** by law. In Latin there are two words for law: *jus, juris,* and *lex, legis. Jus* means right. Law protects rights. The Church views law in this light; hence she calls her *Code of Canon Law, Canonicus Jus. Lex* means to bind. Civil society looks at law in this light, as binding the will, as curbing one's freedom, to protect the weak against the strong and thus insure freedom.

Katherine Lee Bates in "America" saw law as the key to preserving our liberty.

>Confirm thy soul in self-control
>Thy liberty in law.

The Declaration of Independence stated that the purpose of government was "To secure these Rights (to Life, Liberty, and the Pursuit of Happiness) . . . ."

The first ten amendments to the Constitution are simply a Bill of Rights.

The temptation for those who do not have is to steal.

The temptation for those who have is to want more.

Both extremes are bad: to have nothing or everything.

The middle of the road is to *"seek first the kingdom of God and His righteousness, and all these things will be given you besides"* (*Matt.* 6:33).

Chapter 15

Why is it wrong to covet your neighbor's goods?

"To covet," as we have already pointed out, is to want wrongly what another has; it is an unreasonable desire for what belongs to another, springing from envy, avarice, or greed.

Scripture does not say that money is evil, only that the **unreasonable love** of money is evil. *"For the **love** of money,"* said St. Paul, *"is the root of all evil, and some people in their desire for it have strayed from the faith and have pierced themselves with many pains"* (*1 Timothy* 6:10).

The author of *Hebrews* writes: *"Let your life be free from **love** of money but be content with what you have, for he has said, 'I will never forsake you or abandon you'"* (*Heb.* 13:5).

Poison is all right in the bottle, but don't let it get into the bloodstream. Money, too, is all right, but don't let it get into your blood.

For money, Judas sold Jesus (*Matt.* 26:15).

For money, soldiers lied about the Resurrection of Jesus (*Matt.* 28:13).

For money, Ananias and Sapphira lied to the apostles and died on the spot (*Acts* 5:1-11).

Money is behind abortions, drug pushing, pornography.

Jesus likened riches to thorns that can choke out the wheat of virtue (*Matt.* 13:7).

Money has enriched thousands, but has damned tens of thousands.

Francis Bacon in his Essay "Of Riches" says: "I cannot call riches better than the baggage of virtue. The Roman word is better, *impedimenta*. For as the baggage is to an army, so is riches to virtue. It cannot be spared nor left behind, but it hindreth the march; yea, and the care of it sometimes loseth or disturbeth the victory. Of great riches there is no real use, except it be in the distribution; the rest is but conceit."

Money may be the key to everything but Heaven; it may provide everything but happiness. Often in seeking everything that money can buy, we lose everything that money cannot buy.

It behooves us, therefore, to cultivate two virtues:

- First, **detachment**. Blessed are the poor in spirit; not the poor, but the poor in spirit: those detached from wealth. There are no U-hauls behind hearses. We have not here a lasting city. The world is a motel, not our home. Use it, but remember we must pass on. To drive this fact home Jesus told the Parable of the Rich Fool (*Luke* 12:16-21).
- Second, **generosity.** It is in giving that we receive (*Luke* 6:38). Read Jesus' Parable of the Rich Man and Lazarus (*Luke* 16:19-31).

Contrast the Sea of Galilee and the Dead Sea. The Sea of Galilee feeds the Jordan River; it supplies fish for man to make a living; it quenches the thirst of those who dwell on its shores. Its waters sparkle in the sunlight. Our Lord loved this Sea and walked on its waters. The Dead Sea, on the contrary, does not feed any stream; it has no fish to give, nor water to drink. It is a selfish Sea. Because it gives nothing, it has no life—it is dead! Jesus loathed the Dead Sea and avoided it.

The Tenth Commandment says, "Be content." Grow where you are planted. Plough the plot of ground God has given you to plough. That's enough.

Nothing less than God can satisfy the human heart. The eye is not filled with seeing. Solomon surpassed in riches all that were before him in Jerusalem, yet he lamented: *"Vanity of vanity and all is vanity except to love God."*

St. Augustine said that the human heart is triangular and the world is round: it cannot fill the corners of the heart— only the triune God can. So Augustine confessed: "Our hearts, therefore, are restless until they rest in Thee."

Discontentment comes from envy, being sad about the good fortune of another as though it were a reflection on you; and covetousness, always wanting what you don't have.

When Nelson Rockefeller died, the headline in the paper read: "Rockefeller leaves 70 million." That morning I happened to be flying from the Caribbean to the States. A Chicago businessman sat next to me on the plane. He almost became ecstatic with the headline. "Think of it, Father," he said to me, "he left 70 million. What an achievement!" I simply said, "He left it. What about his immortal soul?"

"What profit would there be for one to gain the whole world and forfeit his life?" (*Matt.* 16:26).

Chapter 16

Why is it wrong to tell lies?

A lie is saying something that you know is not true. It is wrong for the simple reason that it is **the abuse of the faculty of speech**. Speech has been given us by Almighty God so that we can build up social relations. Words are the bridges between people. Lies rot the bridges and isolate man. Lies destroy society and intercommunication, for you can't trust a liar.

Furthermore, a lie can harm others. The lie of Satan robbed us of the earthly paradise. In *Othello* the lies of Iago caused the murder of Desdemona. St. Isaac Jogues was tortured and finally murdered by the Iroquois because they believed the lies the Dutch had spread about Catholics.

A lie told to harm another is called **calumny.** Calumny is one of the worst sins against the Eight Commandment. It is against truth, for it is a lie; it is against justice, for it harms another; and it is against charity, for one ought to love his neighbor. The Pharisees brought about the death of Jesus through their calumny—lies—about Him to Pilate.

Calumny hits a person where it hurts most, namely, in his reputation.

In the play, *Othello,* Iago says to Othello:

> A good name in man and woman, dear my Lord,
> Is the immediate jewel of their souls:
> Who steals my purse steals trash
> But he that filches from me my good name

Robs me of that which not enriches him,
And makes me poor indeed (III, 3).

In the case of calumny, it is not enough to confess the sin; restitution must be made, as when you steal. Only here the matter is more serious, because a good name is better than riches.

A malicious gossip came to Confession to St. Philip Neri. Before giving her absolution, Philip gave her as a penance to take a pillow of feathers to the wind. After doing that, the woman came back for her absolution. Philip said, "You've done only half your penance; now go and collect the feathers you scattered." She protested that she could not do this. "So," said Philip, "it is equally impossible to undo the damage your lying tongue has caused."

What may be just as harmful as lying is telling the truth about another when the truth hurts. A young woman moves into a new neighborhood to start life anew. She has had a baby out of wedlock. No one knows, but a busybody. She spreads the word and destroys the woman's chance to get ahead in the area. We label such "backbiting" as the sin of **detraction** or **slander**.

There is so much bad in the best of us,
And so much good in the worst of us,
That it ill behooves any of us
To speak ill of the rest of us.

Never be a person with an orchid face and a cactus tongue.

The basis of so much slander and lying is **rash judgments**. A rash judgment is jumping to conclusions about others. An English lady, a self-appointed supervisor of the morals of the village, accused a workman of having reverted to drink, because "with her own eyes" she had seen his wheelbarrow standing outside a saloon.

The accused man made no verbal defense. That evening he placed his wheelbarrow outside the lady's door and left it there—all night!

Jesus said: *"Stop judging and you will not be judged. Stop condemning and you will not be condemned"* (*Luke* 6:37).

We have no right to judge. We cannot read the human heart. You cannot tell a book by its cover. It is so easy to misconstrue an event. St. Joseph found Mary with child; it looked like adultery. But St. Joseph was a just man; he did not jump to any conclusion. He prayed, and God sent an angel to clear up the problem.

The French have a saying: *Comprendre tout, c'est pardonner tout*—"to know all, is to forgive all." An Indian proverb says: "Don't judge any man until you have walked two moons in his moccasins." Ben Johnson said that "God leaves His judgment to Judgment Day; let us do likewise."

Sometime go to the library and get Mark Hellinger's short story "The Rat." It is a classic example about how wrong people can be in judging another.

The greatest tribute that could be paid to the character of George Washington was in the cherry tree story and the remark: "I cannot tell a lie."

Always tell the truth, no matter the cost. Be sincere!

The word "sincerity" has an interesting origin. In Roman times buildings were made of huge blocks of marble. Sometimes the corner of a block would be chipped off. Rather than discard the block, contractors often filled in the break with wax. No one noticed the replacement until the building was finished; then the discoloration would show, but it would be too late to remove the damaged block. So, contracts had a clause that all the marble in the building be *sine cera;* that is, without any wax. Thus the word "sincere" came to mean pure, genuine, of one consistency.

Some wag said, "Being two-faced never doubled anybody's face value."

"If you blow upon a spark, it quickens into flame. If you spit on it, it dies out. Yet both you do with your mouth!" (*Sirach* 28:12). The tongue can build up or destroy.

St. James says: *"If anyone does not fall short in speech, he is a perfect man"* (3:2-8).

Chapter 17

Epilogue

One day a rich young man approached Jesus and said: *"Teacher, what good must I do to gain eternal life?"* He called Jesus "Teacher." That was a poor start, because "Teacher" was a title used by unbelievers. Still, he came to Jesus, for he felt that Jesus had the answer to life's deepest question, namely, what good must be done to gain eternal life.

Jesus answered him: *"There is only One who is good."* Jesus implied that this One must be loved. Because this One is God, and because God is goodness *par excellence*, this One is above all lovable and to be loved. Therefore, the greatest good is to love Him. He was bringing the young man back to the first table of the Ten Commandments: the love of God.

Then Jesus continued: *"If you wish to enter into life, keep the commandments."* But the man was not satisfied. He asked: *"Which commandments?"* Jesus then lead him to the love of neighbor: the commandments on the second table of the Decalogue. *"You shall not kill,"* Jesus replied. *"You shall not commit adultery; you shall not steal; you shall not bear false witness; honor your father and your mother; and you shall love your neighbor as yourself"* (*Matt.* 19:16-19).

This incident in the life of Jesus teaches us that there is a relationship between doing good and eternal life—that this good is determined by a norm of morality outside ourselves, by none other than God Himself, who alone is good. This norm God expressed in the Old Testament by the Ten Commandments and in the New Testament by the Sermon on the Mount—*"Do not think that I have come to abolish the law or the prophets"* (*Matt.* 5:17).

The rule is simple: to enter into eternal life, keep the commandments! Thus Sirach wrote, there is *"nothing more salutary than to obey His commandments"* (23:27).

Other Books
By Rev. Albert J. M. Shamon

Our Lady Teaches About Prayer at Medjugorje	$3.00
Our Lady Says: Let Holy Mass Be Your Life	$3.00
Our Lady Says: Monthly Confession—	
Remedy for the West	$3.00
Our Lady Teaches About Sacramentals	
and Blessed Objects	$3.00
Our Lady Says: Pray the Creed	$3.00
Three Steps to Sanctity	$3.00
The Power of the Rosary	
English	$3.00
Spanish	$3.00
Our Lady Says: Love People	$5.00
The Ten Commandments of God	$5.00
Behind the Mass	$5.00
Apocalypse—The Book For Our Times	$6.95
Firepower Through Confirmation	$5.95
Genesis: The Book of Origins	$6.95
A Graphic Life of Jesus the Christ	$9.95

For additional information, contact CMJ Marian Publishers, distributor of Catholic books.

Please write to:

CMJ Marian Publishers & Distributors
P.O. Box 661
Oak Lawn, Illinois 60454
www.cmjbooks.com
Toll Free: 888-636-6799
Fax: 708-636-2855